Stacking Pennies

By

Courtney Grub`ert

authorHOUSE™

1663 LIBERTY DRIVE, SUITE 200
BLOOMINGTON, INDIANA 47403
(800) 839-8640
WWW.AUTHORHOUSE.COM

First published by AuthorHouse 01/23/06

ISBN: 1-4184-7029-5 (e)
ISBN: 1-4184-5316-1 (sc)

Printed in the United States of America
Bloomington, Indiana

This book is printed on acid-free paper.

Dear Reader,

The objective of this book is to expound a little on how you can spend less and live like caviar without buying "cheaper things" or changing your life style. I wrote this book because I have been called cheap; however, you can't be called cheap if you have everything. The right term is frugal and only people who know how to budget their money will be the ones to keep it. It doesn't matter how much money you make, if you don't know how to spend it, you will always be broke.

Courtney R. Grub'ert

Dedication

I am honored and proud to acknowledge the contributions of my friends and family.

- To **Elsie Turner** my mom, for all her love and care in helping me to express my creativity.

- To **Columbus Curtis** a good friend, who always told me that I could squeeze a dime out of a nickel?

- To **Catherine Sutherland** a good friend, who inspired me to write this book, and told me that I can accomplish anything in life.

- To **Vincent Davis** for all the love and support over the many years.

<u>*Opening Statement*</u>

Dear Reader,

I am writing this book to give you an understanding on how to make the best of spending and saving money. I am comparing everything as though this were you and your neighbor.

Starting Off

You and Your neighbor both make $50,000.00 a year. He has a Toyota Camry and you have a Ferrari. Now how is this? You know penny pinching and he does not! At the end of this book the comparing sheet will show you how much more money you will have over your neighbor's spending money.

So good luck on saving your money and living the life you have always wanted.

Table of Contents

$$$$ $$$ $$$$ $$$ $$$$ $$$
$$$$

$$$$ $$$$ $$$ $$$$ $$$
$$$$ $$$

$$$$ $$$$ $$$ $$$$ $$$ $$

$$$$ $$$ $$ $$$$ $$$$ $$$

$$$$ $$$ $$ $$$$ $$$ $$$$
$$$ $$$$ $$$ $$$$ $$$

$$$$ $$$$ $$$ $$$$ $$$$
$$$$
$$$ $$$$ $$$ $$

$$$$ $$$ $$$$ $$$ $$$$ $$$
$$$$

$$$$ $$$$ $$$ $$$$ $$$
$$$$ $$$

$$$$ $$$$ $$$ $$$$ $$$ $$

$$$$ $$$ $$ $$$$ $$$$ $$$

$$$$ $$$ $$ $$$$ $$$ $$$$
$$$ $$$$ $$$ $$$$ $$$

$$$$ $$$$ $$$ $$$$ $$$$
$$$$
$$$ $$$$ $$$ $$

$$$$ $$$ $$$$ $$$ $$$$ $$$
$$$$

$$$$ $$$$ $$$ $$$$ $$$
$$$$ $$$

$$$$ $$$$ $$$ $$$$ $$$ $$

$$$$ $$$ $$ $$$$ $$$$ $$$

This book is written to give a better understanding on how to make the best out of spending less.

Good Luck $$$

*M*aking the best out of Spending 'less'
$

$\mathscr{S}$tack $1

How to save money

How to save money:

There are so many ways to save
money.

    1 - By taking your time.

    2 - By comparing prices and
        estimating cost.

    3 - By keeping your receipts.

    4 - By using coupons.

    5 - By keeping all gifts even if you
        don't like them.

    6 - By where you shop.

    7 - Sales.

Making the best out of Spending 'less'
$

Listed below are a few ideas. I have discovered how you can save money.

· Always keep your bankbook balanced, because you never want to be charged an overdraft fee. **Keep at least $30.00 in your savings account.**

· Do not do Layaways if you don't have to, because you are paying an **Extra fee** to hold something.

· Don't forget sales!
Check your Sunday paper for weekly sales.

You do not want to spend any extra money if you don't have to.

*M*aking the best out of Spending 'less'
$

Remember the more pennies you pinch on regular items the more money you save, and that my friend is your caviar money. You'll have extra money to do whatever you like. This is your Versace money. Now you can walk into a Department store and buy that $100.00 Versace shirt you've been dying for. You have earned it by penny pinching. We all want nice things, even if it's just a nice house, car or a new wardrobe. We work hard everyday, so we have the right to enjoy our hard earned money. It is my job to show you how to make the best out of saving and spending your money. So, you can live like caviar with all the extra money you have saved.

Making the best out of Spending 'less'
$

$\mathscr{S}$tack $2

Free Stuff

"Free Stuff"- What stores and
fast food restaurants give you for free?

Napkins	$3.00
Jelly	$1.50
Butter	$1.25
Syrup	$2.00
Sugar	$2.00
Salt	$1.25
Pepper	$2.00
Sweet & Low	$1.00
Ketchup	$1.00
Soy Sauce	$1.50

*M*aking the best out of Spending 'less'
$

Hot Sauce	$1.50
Duck Sauce	$1.50
Plastic Forks	$1.00
Plastic Knives	$1.00
Salad Dressing	$1.50
Mayonnaise	$1.50
Straws	$1.00

Total money saved $25.00

The items you picked up for free. Be reasonable don't take advantage!

*M*aking the best out of Spending 'less'
$

$\mathcal{S}$tack $3

How to get free money from the bank?

Money Market Accounts $

Inestment Account $

You're probably thinking how on earth does a bank give you money? Well, it's easy. Ask your bank what type of account would earn you the most interest on your money. If your bank doesn't have any interest bearing accounts, then you will need to invest in a bank that has interest bearing accounts. My bank pays me $10.00 a month in interest for saving my money in one of their interest bearing accounts. These accounts are designed for you.

*M*aking the best out of
Spending 'less'
$

Never invest your money into any financial institution without knowing the risk of losing it all.

Also, if you have extra money lying around, put it in a CD for a couple of months. You can earn interest on CDs also.

Total = Amount earned in **Free Money** for the year.

$120 dollars

Making the best out of
Spending 'less'
$

$\mathscr{S}$tack $4

What to think about before spending your money?

Always try to purchase the best product at the lowest price. Do not buy a cheap item it may break. Do not buy an expensive item you are spending too much money. If you are like me, in a couple of months you may change your mind, or your style may change.

Example:
- $15 is what you spent on a cheap item
- $15 more is spent trying to replace the cheap item because the first item you bought broke.
- $50 spent on a quality item, and it does not break

*M*aking the best out of Spending 'less'
$

· $150 you spend on the most expensive thing in the store and next month you don't like it anymore or you just decided to remodel your house.

Now you just spent $50 more on the cheap item trying to replace it and you just spent $150.00 on something that you now do not want. So what do you do? Purchase the best quality product at the lowest price. Now you will not have to worry about the cheap item you bought breaking or spending too much on something. This is one more thing to remember when you do buy something. If you realize that you don't like it and you can't return it to the store. Don't panic, save it and give it to someone as a gift for **Christmas, birthdays, or any type of celebration.**

*M*aking the best out of Spending 'less'
$

$$ $$ $$ $$

     $$ $$ $$

$$ $$ $$ $$

$$ $$ $$ $$

     $$ $$ $$

$$ $$ $$ $$

$$ $$ $$ $$

     $$ $$ $$

$$ $$ $$ $$

$$ $$ $$ $$

     $$ $$ $$

$$ $$ $$ $$

Raining Money

*M*aking the best out of Spending 'less'
$

$\mathscr{S}$tack $5

Ideas on how to spend money and where to shop

Example:

- I buy rice at the oriental store WHY? Because I get a 25 Ib bag of jasmine rice for $5.00.

- Compared to a little 16 oz bag of rice at the grocery store for $1.50.

- Buy soap at Wal-Mart or somewhere that won't cost you an arm and a leg.

Sometimes it's better to buy in bulk and sometimes it's not. Always compare prices.

*M*aking the best out of Spending 'less'
$

Example:

- One box of candy consisting of 18 pieces costs $1.00

- One box of candy consisting of 36 pieces costs $3.00

Which one would you get 2 boxes of?

- 18 for only $2.00

- 1 box of 36 for $3.00

Always use every last little bit of everything.

Example: Toothpaste
We use most of it but throw away the last little bit and that adds up over time. You are throwing away money.

Making the best out of Spending 'less'
$

· Most of the time when we go out to eat we throw away the last little bit. Get a doggie bag, take the left over food home and eat it later. It becomes a new meal.

Where you shop has a lot to do with saving money. It doesn't matter how much money you make. If you don't know how to spend it you will always be broke.

Where you shop:

· Don't go to a high price department store for soap, go to Wal-Mart. Why pay $20.00 for soap when you can get it at Wal-Mart for $3.00.

WHY not clean your car yourself. Well, not the whole car because I know sometimes we all can get a little lazy. But if you vacuum your own car that's less money than paying extra when you go to have it fully cleaned.

Making the best out of Spending 'less'
$

- **Cars** - If you don't mind buying a used car go to a **Rent to Own car dealership.** Cars are marked down much lower than they are at a regular price car dealership.

- **Home buying** - 'Go HUD', it's a lot cheaper. A HUD home is simply a home that's vacated and purchased by the government and sold at a reduced rate.

Shop at a stores that gives you a discount card, which will save you money. Example – grocery stores have their own discount cards.

When you see (buy one get one free) go for it. You can think about what to do with it later. If you don't want it you can always give it away as a gift.

*M*aking the best out of Spending 'less'
$

Dollar Stores:

I cannot emphasize or express enough, the savings you will earn by shopping at a Dollar Store. The Dollar Stores have everything. Hair products, office products, school supplies, baby clothes, make-up, ornaments for all seasons, kitchen items, car products, food, candy, tapes, books and basically anything you can possibly think of.

ALL FOR ONLY $1.00!!!!

Other stores that have lower priced items are:

Dollar General, Family Dollar, Big Lots, and if you like named brand clothing and don't want to pay the mall prices, check out A. J. Wright, Ross, and T. J. MAXX (which are my favorite stores). They have the best designer fashion at bargain prices.

*M*aking the best out of
Spending 'less'
$

Coupons:

The savings is terrific. One day I went to K-Mart and purchased some designer luggage for half the price that I would have paid at an expensive department store.

Always refer to the Sunday paper to compare items and prices. That's if you don't want to run from store to store trying to find the best price. Remember the newspaper has a bargain section on the stores in your area. Check it out for the best savings and sale items.

Every week many stores may have certain items on sale.

For Example:
- Best Buy
- Circuit City
- Office Max
- J.C. Penny's
- Target's
- K-Mart

*M*aking the best out of Spending 'less'
$

Prices can be compared from the comfort of your home. Scanning the newspaper saves time, money and headaches.

For those of you who want to save a few more pennies, flea markets, thrift stores and yard sales are a great place to shop and find that special "odd" item.

Making the best out of Spending 'less'
$

$\mathscr{S}$tack $6

Never settle for less.

Buy everything you want, but never settle for less. Always take your time when spending your money. **IF YOU SETTLE FOR LESS THAT IS WHAT YOU WILL GET.** Sometimes when you settle for less you're not happy with what you bought. Now you have to spend more and more money trying to buy something to satisfy that want or that need.

Example:
When I say never settle for less, I mean buy the same soap you always use. **"DO NOT"** buy a cheaper brand of soap, just purchase your soap where it may be less expensive. Shop around. Saving money is the name of the game.

*M*aking the best out of Spending 'less'

$

If you were to spend your money on something that you do not really want. Keep in mind you can always take the item back to the store and get your money back.

- You spend - $500 dollars settling for something.

- You spend - $500 more dollars because you're not satisfied with what you bought.

The money keeps adding up. If you had purchased what you really wanted you would have saved $500 dollars, instead of spending an extra $500. Don't get mad when you overspend on something you no longer want, and can't return it to the store. Keep it and give it away as a gift.

When going out to eat and you find something wrong with your food, do not eat it, send it back.

Making the best out of Spending 'less'
$

Do not settle for less

Always treat yourself as though you are caviar. Send the food back, and in most cases the manager will give you your food for free, or at least a discount. Don't pay for anything that you are not satisfied with.

*M*aking the best out of Spending 'less'
$

$\mathscr{S}$tack $7

Gifts

Gifts are easy:

Keep all the gifts people give you, even if you don't like them. That's ok because now you got a free gift to give to someone else. You saved yourself money on buying someone else a gift.

The more gifts you receive from people the more money you save on not having to buy someone else a gift. You are not being cheap you are simply being economical, So at least the gift someone gave you will now be useful to someone else - you hope!

*M*aking the best out of Spending 'less'
$

Keep Everything:

- Gift bags

- Gift paper

- Gift boxes

Remember every dollar you save adds to your wallet.

*M*aking the best out of Spending 'less'
$

$\mathcal{S}$tack $8

Fast Food

Why I named this stack "fast food".

I am talking about everything that we rush out and overspend on. When eating out only buy what you are going to eat. Don't get the big drink if you can only drink a small one.

Why overspend

You are giving your money away. As my mom would say, "Your eyes are bigger than your stomach".

$$\$\$\$\$\$\$\$$$
$$\$\$\$\$\$$$
$$\$\$\$$$
$$\$$$

*M*aking the best out of
Spending 'less'
$

$\mathscr{S}$tack $9

Taking your time

Take your time when shopping.

First: Plan a day to go shopping. That way you won't have to rush buying something you really don't want.

Shopping: Sometimes it takes at least an hour to walk and look around the entire store. Give yourself enough time to make sure that what you buy is what you really want. If you spend your money on the first thing you see after being in the store for 30 minutes; you may later see something else that you really wanted.

Making the best out of
Spending 'less'
$

Remember always take your time. Give yourself at least an hour to shop. Use this time wisely. Don't cheat yourself. I recommend you list each store that you want to shop in that day and give yourself ample time to shop in each store selected. On the other hand, utilize your time wisely; some stores won't have what you need. It is ok to move onto the next store. If you see something you are really sure about buying, get it. Remember, keep your receipt and if you find a better deal somewhere else later, you can always take it back to the store and get a refund.

Making the best out of Spending 'less'

$

$\mathscr{S}$tack $10

Time Estimation when buying

Clothes: 1 hour or more (depending on how many stores you shop at).

Toothpaste: 1 minute (don't get ridiculous when doing a time estimate. Do what you feel is comfortable for you).

>**Houses:** 6 months
>**Cars:** 2-3 months
>**Home decor:** 2 or more weeks

Give yourself as much time as you need when going to the stores you love to shop at. Make sure you are getting the best price for each item you are looking for. If you can do this in a day, then do so.

*M*aking the best out of Spending 'less'
$

$\mathscr{S}$tack $11

Whenever Possible Economize:

Buy the more expensive pots and pans, because if you buy the least expensive they may break. You have to buy quality or you will end up spending more money replacing them. The quality usually looks better and lasts longer.

Buy cheap when you can buy cheap. Always think about what you are purchasing before buying the item.

Example: - Don't spend $10 on nail polish when $5 nail polish does the same thing.

If you can buy it cheap and it works, go for it. Buy quality when necessary. By thinking first about

*M*aking the best out of Spending 'less'
$

what you have to purchase, you will save yourself money. By doing this, you will always leave your wallet thicker. To have more money is the name of the game.

*M*aking the best out of
Spending 'less'
$

$\mathscr{S}$tack $12

Receipts

Always save your receipts for at least a month. Buying for the sake of buying you may discover that you don't need the item and decide to return it. There is no shame in returning it to the store. The shame is having to spend more money trying to satisfy your need. Remember if you settle for less that is what you will get!

*M*aking the best out of Spending 'less'
$

Example:

- While in a rush you spend $50 dollars on something that you really did not want.

As consumers we have the right to change our mind on anything we buy. Save your receipts for at least one month or longer; so, if you are not satisfied with what you bought return it to the store.

When Traveling:

Always shop at stores that you are familiar with such as national chain stores. More than likely, the same store is in your city, which makes it easier to exchange or get your money back.

Never shop at stores that are not in your city or hometown while traveling, because if you need to return the item you can't. That's wasting your money.

Making the best out of Spending 'less'
$

Example:

- One – you're out of state, it rains, you purchased another umbrella, however, there are three at home.

- Two - it breaks.

- Three - you really didn't like it but you had to have it for that moment.

- Four - you didn't look in the bag and it doesn't have all the pieces.

Now you just wasted $30 on an umbrella (unless you bought it from a store that has a chain in your area and you can take it back) smart thinking!

*M*aking the best out of Spending 'less'
$

Extras

- **Hotels:** Go to a hotel that offers continental breakfast, parking and Internet services. Make sure the hotel offers AAA, military or senior citizen discounts.

- **Cameras:** Only buy from places like Ritz's camera (a chain store) that will gives complimentary items - "free stuff".

- **Example:** Camera bag, cords, disc, software & free pictures.

- **Phone Company:** Only go with a phone company that is going to give you something back.

- **Example:** Some phone companies give blockbuster movie coupons and referral credits. If the service is the same price as the competitors, you may want to go with the company that will give you more for your money.

*M*aking the best out of Spending 'less'
$

- **Credit Cards:** Only go with a credit card company that gives you cash back or frequent flyer miles.

- **Cosmetics:** When buying cosmetics (make up) from a mall or departments store, purchase only the ones that have a free gift. Large department store have lots of gifts with their cosmetic production line.

- **Fix It Centers:** Don't pay a fix it man to come in and change a light bulb because you don't know how too. Go to a Home Improvement Store or Center. They have classes teaching you how to repair objects or items in your home.

*M*aking the best out of
Spending 'less'
$

$\mathscr{S}$tack $13

My Own Examples

Personal examples of how I spend my money.

I eat the Kid's Meal because I eat small. WHY pay for what I don't eat? Prices are subject to change.

Kid's Meal at:

- **ARBY' S**
  Jr. roast beef combo - $1.99
  Adult roast beef combo - $3.99
  I save $2.00

- **WENDY'S**
  Kid's hamburger combo - $ 1.99
  Adult classic single combo - $3.19
  I save $1.20

*M*aking the best out of
Spending 'less'
$

You can shop at different stores to find a better deal. These are just some of my examples.

I go to:
Wal-Mart - for my Caress soap - $2.19 for two bars
Other stores - Caress soap - $2.79 for two bars

I save $ .60 Cents

I purchase the Sunday's paper because it has the most coupons. Coupons may change based on availability of the store.

I always save at least $4 or $5 dollars a week by using my Sunday's paper.

- Hecht's department store has 15% to 20% coupon discounts.

- Michael's Art and Craft 30%, 40% and 50% coupon discounts.

- Paul's Art and Craft 30% 40% and 50% coupon discounts.

*M*aking the best out of Spending 'less'
$

I went into K-Mart's department store. I usually use caress soap, at 2 bars for $2.16. Then I saw Irish Spring was 8 bars for $3.99 (and $3.99 at Wal- Mart) I have said before not to change your personal preferences. However, some deals are too good to pass up.

These were just a few examples. I don't want to bore you with all the things I do. I wrote this book to help you spend less money on what you purchase every day. Now plan a trip to Hawaii with the extra money saved.

$\mathcal{M}$aking the best out of Spending 'less'
$

$\mathscr{S}$tack $14

Saving with coupons and where to buy.

There are many stores that have their own coupons, which is good because whenever you go to that store, you are getting a saving.

I have listed a few stores here, however, there are many more.

1. Bed Bath & Beyond
2. Sears
3. Pizza Hut
4. Hecht's
5. J. C. Penny's
6. Michael's (arts and crafts)
7. Paul's (arts and crafts)
8. Boston Market
9. Taco Bell
10. Glamour Shots (Portraits)

Making the best out of Spending 'less'
$

11. Dry Cleaners (some)
12. Newport News Outlet
13. Eckerd Drug Store
14. Walgreen's
15. Toys R Us
16. Subway
17. Papa John's Pizza

A lot of stores may not have their own coupons but they give good sales, an example: Sports Authority 50% off entire stock of shoes and sandals (they may have coupons but, I haven't seen them).

If you do not normally get the Sunday newspaper buy it just for the coupons. You will earn your money right back just in the savings that you will receive.

*M*aking the best out of Spending 'less'
$

*T*hese are coupons I have seen in my Sunday's paper.

1. L'Oreal mascara	**Save $1.00**
2. Pillsbury cake mix	**Save.50**
3. Pillsbury Brownie mix	**Save.50**
4. Quick mix or Cookie mix	**Save.50**
5. Kid Cuisine	**Save $1.00**
6. Listerine	**Save.75**
7. Puppy Chow	**Save.$1.10**
8. Wisk	**Save $1.00**
9. Snuggle	**Save.40**
10. Snack pack deserts	**Save.40**
11. Martha white (products)	**Save.50**
12. Fiber one	**Save.70**
13. Cocoa & Reese's puffs	**Save.50**
14. Smart Start	**Save $1.00**
15. Oatmeal crisp	**Save $1.00**
Raisin Nut Bran	
Basic 4	
Honey Nut Clusters	
16. Old El Paso Tacos	**Save $1.00**
17. Green Giant Create meal	**Save.50**
18. Green Giant skillet meal	**Save.75**
19. Progresso Soup	**Save.50**

Making the best out of Spending 'less'
$

20. Nestle — **Save.25**
21. Deer Park (water) — **Save $1.00**
22. Clorox BathWand — **Save $1.00**
23. Edge Shaving Gel — **Save $1.00**
24. Tiger Power — **Save $1.00**
25. Crest White strips — **Save $5.00**
26. E.L. Fudge (cookies) — **Save.40**
27. Mazola cooking spray — **Save.30**
28. Colgate — **Save .75**
29. Suave Lotions — **Save .75**
30. Friskies (cat food) — **Save $1.00**
31. Savory Bites (dog snack) — **Save $1.00**
32. Gravy Train (dog snack) — **Save $1.00**
33. Meaty Bone (dog snack) — **Save $1.00**
34. VS Sassoon — **Save $1.00**
35. Caress soap — **Save $1.00**
36. Always — **Save $1.00**
37. Tampax — **Save $1.00**
38. Folgers — **Save $1.00**
39. Slim Fast — **Save $1.00**
40. Downy — **Save .75**
41. Dawn — **Save .30**
42. Bounce — **Save .40**
43. Oil of Olay — **Save $1.00**
44. Safeguard — **Save .25**

Making the best out of Spending 'less' $

45. Zest	**Save .20**
46. Secret deodorant	**Save $1.00**
47. Nice 'n Easy	**Save $2.00**
48. Sure deodorant	**Save $1.00**
49. High endurance body spray	**Save $1.00**
50. Pepto Bismol	**Save $1.00**

Look in the Sunday's newspaper every week; there are more savings each week. The types of coupons vary from week to week.

Make sure you look in your **Community saver** or **Valpak** that is mailed to your home at least once a month. Community Saver coupon packages may vary from city to city. (All cities may not receive these coupon packages).

Coupons that are in your community saver package can be used in your town and elsewhere. I have found discounted airline travel coupons in my community saver. Good luck looking and saving with your community saver.

$\mathcal{M}$aking the best out of
Spending 'less'
$

These are some coupons that I get in my community saver.

- Cottman's Transmission
- Pizza
- Chinese Dining
- Friendly
- Dentist
- Lawn Doctor
- Painting
- Handyman
- House Doctors
- Animal Care
- Childcare
- Auto car wash
- Grease monkey
- Home security system
- Carpet Cleaning

Making the best out of Spending 'less'
$

$\mathscr{S}$tack $15

Savings for "Member's Only"

This is for Automobile Association of America members only, this is not to encourage you to run out and become AAA member if you're not. There are a lot of memberships that you can become a part of that gives you additional savings and coupons.

This savings list is for AAA members only. I added this because there are over 40 million AAA members and I didn't want to eliminate anyone. However, other clubs and memberships offer somewhat of the same deals, so that everyone can get in on the savings.

This list of savings is for AAA members only. See your AAA office for their guide to savings book.

Making the best out of Spending 'less'
$

LODGING, ENTERTAINMENT, RETAIL, TRAVEL

According to the 2005 AAA Guide To Savings you will save 10% or more at these hotels with your AAA membership.

- Comfort Inn
- Comfort Suite
- Quality Inn
- Sleep Inn
- Econo Lodge
- Clarion Hotel
- Main Stay
- Rode Way Inn

These are your Choice Hotels that you here about all the time. AAA has many more hotels that give you a big discount. Best Western, La Quinta, Days Inn, Hyatt Hotels & Resorts.

The Hilton Family:
Hilton, Hampton Inn, Double Tree
Homewood Suites, Embassy
Suites Hotels
Hilton Garden Inn

*M*aking the best out of Spending 'less'
$

The Marriott Family:
Marriott Hotels & Resorts, Residence Inn Renaissance Hotels & Resorts, CourtYard, FairField Inn, TownePlace Suites, SpringHill Suites

The StarWood Family:
Westin, Sheraton, Four Points, St. Regis Luxury Collection, Hotels

Some hotels don't take AAA. You should contact your AAA office to find which ones do not accept AAA. All the ones listed above will take AAA and you will save 10% or more in discounts.

*M*aking the best out of Spending 'less'
$

Dining Entertainment save 10%

Hard Rock Cafe

Joe's Crab Shack

The Crab House

Landry's Seafood House

Entertainment save 10% - 40%

Sea World, Busch Gardens, Sesame Place, Water Country USA, Adventure Island

Universal Orlando

Universal Studios Hollywood

Universal City Walk Orlando

Six Flags Theme Parks

General Cinema

*M*aking the best out of Spending 'less'
$

Retail save 7% & up

Payless Shoes
Some Pharmacy's
Hertz Car sales
NAPA
Lens crafters
Contact lenses
Shop America VIP Casual Corner
Petite Sophisticate
Sunglass Hut
Penske Truck Rental Reebok
Outlet stores
Ralph Lauren Footwear *Outlet*
Greg Norman *Outlet*
stores
Prime Outlet
Tanger Outlet

Travel 10%-25%

Hertz Car Rental, Aloha Airlines Air

Gray Line Tours, Amtrak, Boston Coach

All of these I have listed are just a few, there are many more.

*M*aking the best out of
Spending 'less'
$

$\mathscr{S}$tack $16

Five rules to remember

· Always take your time before spending your money.

· Never settle for what you don't really want.

· Always bargain shop and compare prices.

· Always remember sales.

· Always remember your coupons.

Courtney Grubert

Comparing price sheets

Product	Money spent	Coupons used or compare price	Money saved

Stacking Pennies
*S*tack $1

How to save money

1.

2.

3.

4.

5.

6.

Comparing price sheets

Product	Money spent	Coupons used or compare price	Money saved

Stacking Pennies
Stack $2
<u>Free Money</u>

1.

2.

3.

4.

5.

6.

Comparing price sheets

Product	Money spent	Coupons used or compare price	Money saved

Stacking Pennies
*S*tack $3

How to get free money from the bank?

1.

2.

3.

4.

5.

6.

Comparing price sheets

Product	Money spent	Coupons used or compare price	Money saved

Stacking Pennies
*S*tack $4

<u>What to think about before spending your money?</u>

1.

2.

3.

4.

5.

6.

Comparing price sheets

Product	Money spent	Coupons used or compare price	Money saved

Stacking Pennies
Stack $5

<u>Ideas on how to spend money and where to shop</u>

1.

2.

3.

4.

5.

6.

Comparing price sheets

Product	Money spent	Coupons used or compare price	Money saved

Stacking Pennies
*S*tack $6
Never settle for less.

1.

2.

3.

4.

5.

6.

Comparing price sheets

Product	Money spent	Coupons used or compare price	Money saved

Stacking Pennies
*S*tack $7
<u>Gifts</u>

1.

2.

3.

4.

5.

6.

Comparing price sheets

Product	Money spent	Coupons used or compare price	Money saved

Stacking Pennies
*S*tack $8
<u>Fast Food</u>

1.

2.

3.

4.

5.

6.

Comparing price sheets

Product	Money spent	Coupons used or compare price	Money saved

Stacking Pennies
*S*tack $9
<u>Taking your time</u>

1.

2.

3.

4.

5.

6.

Courtney Grubert

Comparing price sheets

Product	Money spent	Coupons used or compare price	Money saved

Stacking Pennies
*S*tack $10

<u>Time Estimation when buying</u>

1.

2.

3.

4.

5.

6.

Comparing price sheets

Product	Money spent	Coupons used or compare price	Money saved

Stacking Pennies
Stack $11

<u>Whenever Possible Economize:</u>

1.

2.

3.

4.

5.

6.

Courtney Grubert

Comparing price sheets

Product	Money spent	Coupons used or compare price	Money saved

Stacking Pennies
*S*tack $12
<u>Receipts</u>

1.

2.

3.

4.

5.

6.

Comparing price sheets

Product	Money spent	Coupons used or compare price	Money saved

Stacking Pennies
*S*tack $13
<u>My own Examples</u>

1.

2.

3.

4.

5.

6.

Courtney Grubert

Comparing price sheets

Product	Money spent	Coupons used or compare price	Money saved

Stacking Pennies
*S*tack $14

<u>Saving with coupons and where to buy.</u>

1.

2.

3.

4.

5.

6.

Comparing price sheets

Product	Money spent	Coupons used or compare price	Money saved

Stacking Pennies
*S*tack $15
<u>Savings for members only</u>

1.

2.

3.

4.

5.

6.